Do you know what your children are texting?

Do you know what your children are texting?

The Text to English Dictionary

By Jo Anne Dailey

Dailey Publishing

Dedication

For my Husband Greg Dailey, who allows me to flow wherever my imagination takes me!

Acknowledgements

Dr. Gregory Ramey for his knowledge and contribution

My son Ross Hensley who believes I can do anything

My son Austin Hensley who is defending our Nation and my right to pen this book

Jim Ventura for paving the path

Steve Cribbett for being such a good friend

Stewie B. Dailey for inspiration

~ Warning ~

This book contains adult language

Introduction

Oftentimes we feel safe in the belief that our children are safe in our living rooms happily texting away on cell phones to their friends across America. The question is, "Are they really?" Recent studies have shown that predators are now preying on our Nations children by text messaging. Text messaging technology has also developed its own "shorthand" over the years and some of the acronyms are can be very sexually explicit. This book should be on every parent of a teenager's shelf to periodically check the messages your child is sending, receiving and storing in their quick messages.

Below is the complete article written by Dr. Gregory Ramey featured on the back cover.

Do you know what your kids are saying?
Learn about using text messaging to communicate with your children

"when wil u b home 2nite"

"idk I have 2 work"

"k cal me when u r off"

"k l8er"

Do you have any idea what that means?

That was a typical text message exchange between two teens, which translates to:

"When will you be home tonight?"

"I don't know. I have to work."

"Okay. Call me when you are off."

"Okay. Later."

Though a number of parents are not familiar with text messaging, Greg Ramey, PhD, child psychologist at The Children's Medical Center of Dayton, says that it is a skill all parents should learn.

"Parents may not like using text messages to communicate, but they need to realize that this technology is here to stay," says Dr. Ramey.

"Embracing this technology will make it easier to communicate with your children."

Text messaging makes communication easier by allowing parents and children to send text messages quickly with comments like, "I'm home. Luv u."

Dr. Ramey also points out that parents who send text messages to their children instead of calling them all the time is less embarrassing for the child.

"Texting allows for a subtle way for a child to let his or her parents know what is happening, when they will be home or who they are with," says Dr. Ramey.

These little text message reminders can calm a parent's nerves in scary situations. If, for example, a school shooting occurs, children can text their parents to let them know they are safe.

A growing trend at many schools and universities nationwide is a text message alert system where students, faculty and employees sign up and opt in to receive text alerts by providing their cell phone numbers. After the recent shootings at Virginia Tech and Northern Illinois, school administrators feel this form of communication is critical to reach students anytime and anywhere.

Text messaging is also being used to communicate sports scores or notification that grades have been posted online. The advantage of text messaging vs. e-mail is that students are constantly looking at their cell phones.

Text messaging can make certain situations easier, like asking someone on a date. By texting questions or comments instead of talking directly face-to-face, Dr. Ramey says that some children may communicate more. However, he warns that when sharing bad or difficult news, face-to-face communication is always better.

Another way children can use text messaging is for social change. There are groups that send information about volunteer opportunities, eco-friendly tips and other important causes. You and your child can use text messaging to get involved with an important cause; www.mobileactive.org is a great example of an organization using technology to make a difference.

Technology is always changing, but parents have access to great teachers: their children.

"Children can teach this technology easily because they use it everyday," says Dr. Ramey.

"Parents can learn to use the programs, shortcuts and the 'cool' lingo."

As for when a child should have a cell phone, Dr. Ramey says there is no set age. It's completely up to the parents to know if their child is mature enough to handle the responsibility.

"The average age for children to get a cell phone is around junior high," he says. "But make sure they are old enough to understand proper cell phone etiquette."

Dr. Ramey stresses that parents need to explain the proper protocol for cell phones and text messaging.

He advises children and adults to follow these rules:

- Don't text during family meals.
- Show respect during family events, like church and parties, and stay away from the cell phone.
- Don't use text messages to bully others.
- Difficult conversations, like breaking up with a girlfriend or boyfriend and having to tell someone bad news, should be handled face-to-face and at the appropriate time.

"New technology can be scary, but it isn't going away" says Dr. Ramey.

"Parents need to learn how to embrace it in order to stay in touch with their children."

Text messaging shorthand

:P	sticking out my tongue
:)	smiling
: (	frown or sad
;)	wink
;S	hmm? or what?
!	I have a comment
?	I have a question
?	I don't understand what you mean
?4U	question for you
@TEOTD	at the end of the day
\M/	heavy metal music
^5	high five
^RUP^	read up please
^URS	up yours
<3	heart
<33	bigger heart
.02	your (or my) two cents worth
1174	nude club
121	one to one
1337	elite
143	I love you
14AA41	one for all and all for one
182	I hate you
19	zero hand
1DR	I wonder
20	location
2B OR NOT 2B	to be or not to be
2BZ4UQt	too busy for you cutie
2G2B4G	too good to be forgotten
2G2BT	too good to be true
2MI	too much information
2MORO	tomorrow
2NTE	tonight

2U2	to you too
4	for
404	I haven't a clue
411	information
420	marijuana or lets get high
459	I love you
4COL	for crying out loud
4EAE	for ever and ever
4EVER	forever
4NR	foreigner
4Q	fuck you
555	sobbing or crying
55555	crying your eyes out
5FS	5 finger salute
6Y	sexy
8	oral sex
831	I love you
86	out of, over, to get rid of or kicked out
88	bye bye
9	parent is watching
99	parent is no longer watching

A

A/S/L/P	age / sex / location / picture
A3	anyplace, anywhere, anytime
AA	as above
AAF	as a friend
AAK	asleep at keyboard or alive and kicking
AAMOF	as a matter of fact
AAMOI	as a matter of interest
AAP	always a pleasure
AAR	at any rate
AAR8	at any rate
AAS	alive and smiling
AASHTA	as always Sheldon has the answer
AATK	always at the keyboard
AAYF	as always, your friend
AB	ass backwards
ABITHIWTITB	a bird in the hand is worth two in the bush
ABT	about
ABT2	about to
ABTA	goodbye
ACD	alt control delete
ACDNT	accident
ACE	access control entry
ACK	acknowledgement
ACORN	a completely obsessive really nutty person
ACPT	accept
ACQSTN	acquisition
ADAD	another day another dollar
ADBB	all done bye bye
ADD	address
ADIH	another day in hell

17

ADIP	another day in paradise
ADN	advanced digital network or any day now
ADR	address
ADDY	address
ADMIN	administrator
ADMINR	administrator
ADN	any day now
ADR	address
AEAP	as early as possible
AF	April fools
AFAGAY	a friend as good as you
AIAA	as far as I am aware
AFAHMASP	a fool and his money are soon parted
AFAIC	as far as I'm concerned
AFAICS	as far as I can see
AFAICT	as far as I can tell
AFAIK	as far as I know
AFAIR	as far as I remember
AFAIU	as far as I understand
AFAIUI	as far as I understand it
AFAP	as far as possible
AFAYC	as far as you're concerned
AFC	away from computer
AFDN	any fucking day now
AFGO	another fucking growth opportunity
AFIAA	as far as I am aware
AFINIAFI	a friend in need is a friend indeed
AFJ	April fools joke
AFK	away from keyboard or a free kill
AFPOE	a fresh pair of eyes
AFT	about fucking time
AFZ	acronym free zone
AGB	almost good bridge
AGKWE	and god knows what else

AH	at home
AIAMU	and I'm a monkey's uncle
AIGHT	all right
AIH	as it happens
AIMB	as I mentioned before
AIMP	always in my prayers
AIR	as I remember
AISB	as I said before
AISB	as it should be
AISE	as I said earlier
AISI	as I see it
AITR	adult in the room
AKA or A.K.A.	also known as
ALAP	as late as possible
ALCON	all concerned
ALOL	actually laughing out loud
ALOTBSOL	always look on the bright side of life
ALTG	act locally, think globally
AMAP	as many as possible or as much as possible
AMBW	all my best wishes
AMF	adios mother fucker
AML	all my love
AMOF	as a matter of fact
AMRMTYFTS	all my roommates thank you for the show
ANFAWFOS	and now for a word from our sponsor
ANFSCD	and now for something completely different
ANGB	almost nearly good bridge
AOAS	all of a sudden
AOB	abuse of bandwidth
AOE	area of effect
AON	apropos of nothing
AOM	age of mythology or age of majority

19

AOTA	all of the above
AOYP	Angel on your pillow
AP	apple pie
APAC	all praise and credit
AQAP	as quick as possible or as quite as possible
AS	ape shit or another subject
ASAFP	as soon as fucking possible
ASAMOF	as a matter of fact
ASAP	as soon as possible
ASAYGT	as soon as you get this
ASIG	as soon as possible
ASL	age/sex/location
ASLA	age/sex/location /availability
ASLMH	age / sex / location / music / hobbies
AT	at your terminal
ATB	all the best
ATAB	ain't that a bitch
ATC	any two cards
ATEOTD	at the end of the day
ATM	at the moment
ATSITS	all the stars in the sky
ATSL	along the same line
ATST	at the same time
ATW	all the web or around the web
ATWD	agree that we disagree
AWC	after while, crocodile
AWESO	awesome
AWGTHTGTTA	are we going to have to go through this again
AWHFY	are we having fun yet?
AWLTP	avoiding work like the plague
AWNIAC	all we need is another chair
AWOL	absent without leave
AWTTW	a word to the wise

AYC	aren't you clever or aren't you cheeky
AYCE	all you can eat
AYDY	are you done yet?
AYEC	at your earliest convenience
AYK	as you know
AYOR	at your own risk
AYSOS	are you stupid or something
AYS	are you serious?
AYT	are you there?
AYTMTB	and you're telling me this because
AYV	are you vertical?
AZN	Asian

B

B	back
B&F	back and forth
B/C	because
B/F	boyfriend
B/G	background
B2W	back to work
B4	before
B4N	bye for now
B4U	before you
B4YKI	before you know it
B8	bait (underage or joking and teasing)
B9	boss is watching
BA	bad ass
BAC	bad ass chick
BAG	busting a gut or big ass grin
BAK	back at keyboard
BARB	buy abroad but rent in Britain
BAS	big 'butt' smile
BAU	business as usual
BAY	back at ya
BB	be back or baby
BB4N	bye bye for now
BBAMFIC	big bad ass mother fucker in charge
BBB	bye bye babe or boring beyond belief
BBC	big bad challenge
BBBG	bye bye be good
BBFBBM	body by Fisher, brains by Mattel
BBFN	bye bye for now
BBIAB	be back in a bit
BBIAF	be back in a few
BBIAM	be back in a minute
BBIAS	be back in a sec

BBIAW	be back in a while
BBL	be back later
BBMFIC	big bad mother fucker in charge
BBN	bye bye now
BBQ	barbeque
BBR	burnt beyond repair
BBS	be back soon or bulletin board service
BBSD	be back soon darling
BBSL	be back sooner or later
BBT	be back tomorrow
BBW	big beautiful woman
BC	because or be cool
B/C	because
BCBG	bon chic bon genre or belle cu belle geulle
BCBS	big company, big school
BCNU	be seeing you
BCOZ	because
BD	big deal or baby dance or brain drain
BDAY	birthday
B-DAY	birthday
BDBI5M	busy daydreaming back in 5 minutes
BDC	big dumb company or big dot com
BDN	big damn number
BEG	big evil grin
BEOS	nudge
BF	boyfriend or best friend or bitch features
BF2	battlefield 2
BFAW	best friend at work
BFD	big fucking deal
BFE	bum fuck Egypt
BFF	best friends forever
BFFL	best friends for life
BFFLNMW	best friends for life, no matter what
BFFN	best friends for now

BFFTTE	best friends forever till the end
BFE	bumble fuck Egypt
BFG	big fucking grin
BFN	bye for now
BFR	big fucking rock
BFTD	best friends till death
BG	big grin
BGWM	be gentle with me
BHAG	big hairy audacious goal
BHG	big hearted guy or big hearted girl
BHIMBGO	bloody hell, I must be getting old
BHL8	be home late
BHOF	bald headed old fart
BI5	back in five
BIB	boss is back
BIBI	bye bye
BIBO	beer in, beer out
BIF	basis in fact or before I forget
BIL	brother-in-law
BIOIYA	break it off in your ass
BION	believe it or not
BIOYE	blow it out your ear
BIOYIOP	blow it out your I/O port
BIOYN	blow it out your nose
BISFLATM	boy, I sure feel like a turquoise monkey!
BITCH	basically in the clear homey
BITD	back in the day
BITFOB	bring it the fuck on, bitch
BJ	blow job
BJJDI	Billy Joel just drove in
BKA	better known as
BL	belly laughing
BLBBLB	back like bull, brain like bird
BLNT	better luck next time
BM	byte me

BME	based on my experience
BMF	bad mother fucker
BMGWL	busting my gut with laughter
BMOF	bite me old fart
BMOTA	byte me on the ass
BM&Y	between you and me
BNDN	been nowhere done nothing
BNF	big name fan
BO	bug off or body odor
BOB	battery operated boyfriend
BOBFOC	body off Baywatch, face off
BOCTAAE	but of course there are always exceptions
BOFH	bastard operator from hell
BOHICA	bend over here it comes again
BOL	best of luck
BOLO	be on the look out
BOOMS	bored out of my skull
BON	believe it or not
BOSMKL	bending over smacking my knee laughing
BOTEC	back of the envelope calculation
BOTOH	but on the other hand
BOYF	boyfriend
BPLM	big person little mind
BR	bathroom
BRB	be right back
BRD	bored
BRT	be right there
BS	big smile or bull shit or brain strain
BSAAW	big smile and a wink
BSBD&NE	book smart, brain dead & no experience
BSEG	big shit eating grin
BSF	but seriously, folks

BSOD	blue screen of death
BT	byte this
BTA	but then again or before the attacks
BTDT	been there done that
BTDTGTS	been there, done that, got the t-shirt
BTFO	back the fuck off or bend the fuck over
BTHOOM	beats the heck out of me
BTN	better than nothing
BTOIYA	be there or it's your ass
BTSOOM	beats the shit out of me
BTTT	back to the top or bump to the top
BTW	by the way
BTWBO	be there with bells on
BTWITIAILW/U	by the way I think I am in love with you
BW	best wishes
BWDIK	but what do I know
BWL	bursting with laughter
BWO	black, white or other
BYKT	but you knew that
BYOA	bring your own Advil
BYOB	bring your own bottle or bring your own beer
BYOC	bring your own computer
BYOP	bring your own paint (paintball)
BYOW	build your own website or bring your own wine
BYTM	better you than me
BZ	busy

C

C&G	chuckle and grin
C/P	cross post
C/S	change of subject
C4N	ciao for now
CAAC	cool as a cucumber
CAD	Canada or Canadian
CAD	Control, Alt, Delete
CAM	camera
CAS	crack a smile or clear as shit
CB	chat brat or coffee break
CB	crazy bitch
CBB	can't be bothered
CBF	can't be fucked
CBJ	covered blow job
CD9	code 9 - parents are around
CF	coffee freak
CFV	call for vote
CHA	click here asshole
CIAO	goodbye (in Italian)
CICO	coffee in, coffee out
CICYHW	can I copy your home work
CID	consider it done or crying in disgrace
CIS	CompuServe Information Service
CLAB	crying like a baby
CLM	career limiting move
CM	call me
CMAP	cover my ass partner
CMF	count my fingers
CMIIW	correct me if I'm wrong
CMON	come on
CMU	crack me up
CNP	continued in next post

COB	close of business
COD	change of dressing
COF$	Church of Scientology
COFS	Church of Scientology
COS	change of subject
C-P	sleepy
C/P	cross post
CP	chat post
CR8	create
CRAFT	can't remember a fucking thing
CRAP	cheap redundant assorted products
CRAT	can't remember a thing
CRAWS	can't remember anything worth a shit
CRB	come right back
CRBT	crying real big tears
CRDTCHCK	credit check
CRS	can't remember shit
CRTLA	can't remember the three letter acronym
CS	career suicide
CSA	cool sweet awesome
CSL	can't stop laughing
CSN	chuckle, snicker, grin
CSS	counter strike source
CT	can't talk
C-T	city
CTA	call to action
CTC	choking the chicken or care to chat
CTHU	cracking the hell up
CTO	check this out
CU	see you or cracking up
CU2	see you too
CUA	see you around
CUATU	see you around the universe
CUL	see you later

CUL8R	see you later
CULA	see you later alligator
CUMID	see you in my dreams
CUNS	see you in school
CUOL	see you online
CURLO	see you around like a doughnut
CUWTA	catch up with the acronyms
CUZ	because
CWOT	complete waste of time
CWYL	chat with you later
CX	cancelled
CY	calm yourself
CYA	cover your ass or see ya
CYAL8R	see you later
CYE	check your email
CYEP	close your eyes partner
CYL	see you later
CYM	check your mail
CYO	see you online
CYT	see you tomorrow

D

D2	dedos (fingers in Spanish)
D46?	down for sex?
D&M	deep & meaningful
DA	the
DAMHIKT	don't ask me how I know that
DARFC	ducking and running for cover
DBA	doing business as
DBABAI	don't be a bitch about it
DBAU	doing business as usual
DBD	don't be dumb
DBEYR	don't believe everything you read
DD	due diligence or dear daughter
DDD	direct distance dial
DDSOS	different day, same old shit
DEF	definitely
DEGT	dear or darling daughter
DETI	don't even think it
DF	dear friend
DFLA	disenhanced four letter acronym (that is a TLA)
DGA	don't go anywhere
DGAF	don't give a fuck
DGT	don't go there
DGTG	don't go there girlfriend
DGYF	damn girl you're fine
DH	dear husband
DHU	dinosaur hugs
DHYB	don't hold your breath
DIAF	die in a fire
DIC	drunk in charge
DIIK	darned if I know
DIKU	do I know you

DILLIGAD	do I look like I give a damn
DILLIGAF	do I look like I give a fuck?
DILLIGAS	do I look like I give a shit
DINK	double incomes, no kids
DIRFT	do it right the first time
DIS	did I say?
DISTO	did I say that out loud?
DITR	dancing in the rain
DITYID	did I tell you I'm distressed
DIY	do it yourself
DKDC	don't know don't care
DL	download or dead link
D/L	down low
DLBBB	don't let bed bugs bite
DLTBBB	don't let the bed bugs bite
DLTM	don't lie to me
DM	doesn't matter
DMI	don't mention it
DN	down
DNBL8	do not be late
DNC	does not compute
DND	do not disturb
DNR	dinner
DOC	drug of choice
D00D	dude
DOE	depends on experience or daughter of Eve
DOEI	goodbye (in Dutch)
DORD	department of redundancy department
DP	domestic partner
DP	display picture
DPS	damage per second
DPUP	don't poop your pants
DQMOT	don't quote me on this
DQYDJ	don't quit your day job

31

DR	didn't read
DRIB	don't read if busy
DS	dear or darling son
DSTR8	damn straight
DTC	deep throaty chuckle
DTR	define the relationship
DTRT	do the right thing
DTS	don't think so
DUI	driving under the influence
DUM	do you masturbate?
DUNA	don't use no acronyms
DUPE	duplicate
DUR	do you remember
DURS	damn you are sexy
DUSL	do you scream loud?
DUST	did you see that
DV8	deviate
DW	dear or darling wife
DWB	don't write back
DWBH	don't worry be happy
DWF	divorced white female
DWI	driving while intoxicated
DWM	divorced white male
DWPKOTL	deep wet passionate kiss on the lips
DWS	driving while stupid
DWWWI	surfing the world wide web while intoxicated
DWYM	does what you mean
DXNRY	dictionary
DYFM	dude you fascinate me
DYHAB	do you have a boyfriend
DYHAG	do you have a girlfriend
DYJHIW	don't you just hate it when...
DYNWUTB	do you know what you are talking about?

DYOFDW	do your own fucking dirty work
DYOR	do your own research
DYSTSOTT	did you see the size of that thing

E

E	ecstasy or enemy
E1	everyone
E123	easy as one, two, three
E2EG	ear to ear grin
EAK	eating at keyboard
EBKAC	error between keyboard and chair
ED	erase display
EE	electronic emission
EF4T	effort
EFFIN	fucking
EFT	electronic funds transfer
EG	evil grin
EIP	editing in progress
EF4T	effort
EL	evil laugh
EM	excuse me
EMA	e-mail address
EMFBI	excuse me for butting in
EMI	excuse my ignorance
EML	email me later
EMRTW	evil monkey's rule the world
EMSG	e-mail message
ENUF	enough
EOD	end of day or end of discussion
EOL	end of life
EOM	end of message
EOT	end of thread (end of discussion)
ES	erase screen
ESAD	eat shit and die
ESADYFA	eat shit and die you fucking asshole
ESEMED	every second, every minute, every day
ESH	experience, strength, and hope

ESMF	eat shit mother fucker
ESO	equipment smarter than operator
ETA	estimated time of arrival or edited to add
ETLA	extended three letter acronym (that is, an FLA)
EVA	ever
EVO	evolution
EVRE1	everyone
EWG	evil wicked grin
EWI	e-mailing while intoxicated
EZ	easy
EZY	easy

F

F	female
F2F	face to face
F2P	free to play
FAB	features attributes benefits
FAF	funny as fuck
FAH	fucking a hot
FAP	fucking a pissed
FAQL	frequently asked questions list
FAQOMFT	frequently argued waste of my fucking time
FASB	fast ass son bitch
FAWC	for anyone who cares
FB	fuck buddy
FBF	fat boy food
FBI	fucking brilliant idea or female body inspector
FBKS	failure between keyboard and seat
FBM	fine by me
FC	fingers crossed
FCFS	first come, first served
FC'INGO	for crying out loud
FDGB	fall down go boom
FE	fatal error
FEITCTAJ	fuck 'em if they can't take a joke
FF	friends forever
FF&PN	fresh fields and pastures new
FFS	for fuck sake
FGDAI	fahgedaboudit or forget about it
FICCL	frankly I couldn't care less
FIF	fuck I'm funny
FIIK	fuck if I know
FIIOOH	forget it, I'm out of here

FIL	father-in-law
FILF	father I'd like to fuck
FILTH	failed in London, try Hong Kong
FIMH	forever in my heart
FINE	fucked up, insecure, neurotic & emotional
FISH	first in, still here
FITB	fill in the blanks
FLA	four letter acronym
FLUID	fucking look it up, I did
FMLTWIA	fuck me like the whore I am
FMTYEWTK	far more than you ever wanted to know
FMUTA	fuck me up the ass
FNG	fucking new guy
FO	fuck off
FOAD	fuck off and die
FOAF	friend of a friend
FOAG	fuck off and Google
FOC	free of charge
FOFL	falling on floor laughing
FOL	fond of leather
FOMC	fell off my chair
FOMCL	falling off my chair laughing
FORD	found on road dead or fixed or repaired daily or fucked over rebuilt dodge
FOS	full of shit
FRED	fucking ridiculous electronic device
FRT	for real though
FS	for sale
FSBO	for sale by owner
FSR	for some reason
FSU	fuck shit up
FTASB	faster than a speeding bullet
FTBOMH	from the bottom of my heart
FTF	fuck that's funny or face to face

FTFOI	for the fun of it or for the fuck of it
FTL	faster than light
FTLOG	for the love of god
FTN	fuck that noise
FTR	for the record
FTRF	fuck that's really funny
FTTB	for the time being
FTW	for the win or fuck the world
FU2	fuck you too
FUBAR	fucked up beyond all recognition
FUBB	fucked up beyond belief
FUD	fear, uncertainty and disinformation
FUJIMO	fuck you jack I'm moving' on
FUM	fucked up mess
FURTB	filled up and ready to burst
FW	forward
FWB	friends with benefits
FWD	forward
FWIW	for what it's worth
FYA	for your amusement
FYE	for your edification
FYEO	for your eyes only
FYF	from your friend
FYI	for your information
FYIFV	fuck you I'm fully vested
FYLTGE	from your lips to god's ears
FYM	for your misinformation
FYSBIGTBABN	fasten your seatbelts it's going to be a bumpy night

G

G	guess or grin or giggle
G/F	girlfriend
G1	good one
G2CU	good to see you
G2G	got to go
G2GLYS	got to go love ya so
G2R	got to run
G4I	go for it
G4N	good for nothing
G9	genius
GA	go ahead
GAB	getting a beer
GAL	get a life
GALGAL	give a little get a little
GALHER	get a load of her
GALHIM	get a load of him
GANB	getting another beer
GAP	got a pic or gay ass people
GAS	got a second
GB	good bridge
GBG	great big grin
GBH	great big hug
GBU	God Bless You
GC	good crib
GD&R	grinning, ducking and running
GD&RF	grinning, ducking and running fast
GDI	god damn it or god damn independent
GDW	grin, duck and wave
GF	girlfriend
GFF	go fucking figure
GFI	go for it
GFN	gone for now

GFON	good for one night
GFR	grim file reaper
GFTD	gone for the day
GFY	good for you or go fuck yourself or go find yourself
GFYMF	go fuck yourself mother fucker
GG	good game or gotta go
GGA	good game all
GGN	gotta go now
GGOH	gotta get out of here
GGP	gotta go pee
GH	good hand
GI	google it
GIAR	give it a rest
GIC	gift in crib
GIDK	gee I don't know
GIGO	garbage in, garbage out
GIRL	guy in real life
GIWIST	gee, I wish I'd said that
GJ	good job
GJP	good job partner
GL	good luck or get lost
GLA	good luck all
GLBT	gay, lesbian, bisexual, transgender
GLG	good looking girl
GLGH	good luck and good hunting
GL/HF	good luck, have fun
GLNG	good luck next game
GLYASDI	God loves you and so do I
GM	good morning or good move
GMAB	give me a break
GMAFB	give me a fucking break
GMBA	giggling butt off
GMTA	great minds think alike
GMTFT	great minds think for themselves

GN	good night
GNBLFY	got nothing but love for you
GNIGHT	good night
GNITE	good night
GNOC	get naked on cam
GNSD	good night sweet dreams
GOI	get over it
GOK	god only knows
GOL	giggling out loud
GOS	gay or straight
GOWI	get on with it
GOYHH	get off your high horse
GR&D	grinning running and ducking
GR2BR	good riddance to bad rubbish
GR8	great
GRATZ	congratulations
GRL	girl
GRRR	growling
GRWG	get right with God
GSOAS	go sit on a snake
GSOH	good sense of humor
GSYJDWURMNKH	good seeing you, just don't wear your monkey hat
GT	good try
GTFO	get the fuck out
GTFOOH	get the fuck out of here
GTG	got to go
GTGB	got to go, bye
GTGP	got to go pee
GTH	go to hell
GTK	good to know
GTM	giggle to myself
GTRM	going to read mail
GTSY	glad to see you
GUD	geographically undesirable

GWI	get with it
GWS	get well soon
GYHOOYA	get your head out of your ass
GYPO	get your pants off

H

H8	hate
H8TTU	hate to be you
H&K	hugs and kisses
H/C	how come
H/O	hold on
H/P	hold please
H4U	hot for you
H4XX0R	hacker or to be hacked
HAGD	have a great day
HAGN	have a good night
HAGO	have a good one
HAGT	have a good time
HAK	hugs and kisses
HAND	have a nice day
HAR	hit and run
HAU	how about you?
HAWTLW	hello and welcome to last week
HB	hurry back
HBASTD	hitting bottom and starting to dig
HBB	hip beyond belief
HBIB	hot but inappropriate boy
H-BDAY	happy birthday
HBU	how about you?
HCC	holy computer crap
HD	hold
HF	hello friend or have fun or have faith
HFAC	holy flipping animal crackers
H-FDAY	Happy Fathers Day
HHIS	hanging head in shame
HHO1/2K	ha ha, only half kidding
HHOJ	ha-ha, only joking
HHOK	ha ha, only kidding

HHOS	ha-ha, only serious
HHTYAY	happy holidays to you and yours
HIG	how's it going
HIH	hope it helps
HIOOC	help, I'm out of coffee
HITAKS	hang in there and keep smiling
HL	half life
HLA	hola / hello
H-MDAY	happy mother's day
HMFIC	head mofo in charge
HNL	whole 'nother level
HNTI	how nice that/this is
HNTW	how nice that was
HNY	happy new year
HO	hold on
HOAS	hold on a second
HOHA	Hollywood hacker
HOIC	hold on, I'm coming
HOYEW	hanging on your every word
HP	higher power or hit points or health points
HPPO	highest paid person in office
HRU	how are you?
HSIK	how should I know
HT	hi there
HTB	hang the bastards
HTH	hope this (or that) helps
HTNOTH	hit the nail on the head
HUA	heads up ace or head up ass
HUB	head up butt
HUGZ	hugs
HUYA	head up your ass
HV	have
HW	homework
HWGA	here we go again

I 1-D-R	I wonder
I2	I too or me too
I&I	intercourse & inebriation
IA8	I already ate
IAC	in any case or I am confused
IAE	in any event
IAITS	it's all in the subject
IANAC	I am not a crook
IANADBIPOOTV	I am not a doctor but I play one on TV
IANAE	I am not an expert
IANAL	I am not a lawyer
IANNNGC	I am not nurturing the next generation of casualties
IASAP4U	I always say a prayer for you
IAT	I am tired
IAW	I agree with or in accordance with
IAYM	I am your master
IB	I'm back
IBGYBG	I'll be gone, you'll be gone
IBIWISI	I'll believe it when I see it
IBK	idiot behind keyboard
IBRB	I'll be right back
IBT	in between technology
IBTC	itty bitty titty committee
IBTD	I beg to differ
IBTL	in before the lock
IC	in character or I see
ICAM	I couldn't agree more
ICBW	I could be wrong or it could be worse
ICDI	I can't even discuss it
ICFILWU	I could fall in love with you

ICYC	in case you're curious or in case you care
ID10T	idiot
IDC	I don't care
IDGAF	I don't give a fuck
IDGARA	I don't give a rat's ass
IDGI	I don't get it or I don't get involved
IDK	I don't know
IDK, MY BFF JILL	I don't know, my best friend forever Jill
IDKY	I don't know you
I-D-L	ideal
IDM	it does not matter
IDST	I didn't say that
IDTA	I did that already
IDTS	I don't think so
IDUNNO	I don't know
IEF	it's Esther's fault
IF/IB	in the front or in the back
IFAB	I found a bug
IFU	I fucked up
IG2R	I got to run
IGGP	I gotta go pee
IGHT	I got high tonight
IGN	I've got nothing
IGTP	I get the point
IHA	I hate acronyms
IHAIM	I have another instant message
IHNO	I have no opinion
IHTFP	I have truly found paradise or I hate this fucking place
IHU	I hear you or I hate you
IIABDFI	if it ain't broke, don't fix it
IIIO	Intel inside, idiot outside
IIMAD	if it makes any difference

IIR	if I remember or if I recall
IIRC	if I remember correctly or if I recall correctly
IIT	is it tight?
IITLYTO	if it's too loud you're too old
IITYWIMWYBMAD	if I tell you what it means will you buy me a drink
IITYWYBMAD	if I tell you will you buy me a drink
IIWM	if it were me
IJPMP	I just pissed my pants
IJWTK	I just want to know
IJWTS	I just want to say
IK	I know
IKALOPLT	I know a lot of people like that
IKR	I know, right?
IKWYM	I know what you mean
IKYABWAI	I know you are but what am I?
ILBL8	I'll be lat
ILA	I love acronyms
ILF/MD	I love female/male dominance
ILICISCOMK	I laughed, I cried, I spat/spilt coffee/crumbs/coke on my keyboard
ILU	I love you
ILUAAF	I love you as a friend
ILUM	I love you man
ILY	I love you
IM	instant messaging or immediate message
IM2BZ2P	I am too busy to (even) pee
IMA	I might add
IMAO	in my arrogant opinion
IMCO	in my considered opinion
IME	in my experience
IMEZRU	I am easy, are you?

IMHEIUO	in my high exalted informed unassailable opinion
IMHO	in my humble opinion
IML	I love you
IMNERHO	in my never even remotely humble opinion
IMNSHO	in my not so humble opinion
IMO	in my opinion
IMOO	in my own opinion
IMPOV	in my point of view
IMRU	I am, are you?
IMS	I am sorry
IMSB	I am so bored
IMTM	I am the man
IMU	I miss you
INAL	I'm not a lawyer
INBD	it's no big deal
INMP	it's not my problem
INNW	if not now, when
INPO	in no particular order
INUCOSM	it's no use crying over spilt milk
IOH	I'm outta here
IOMH	in over my head
ION	index of names
IOUD	inside, outside, upside down
IOW	in other words
IPN	I'm posting naked
IRL	in real life
IRMC	I rest my case
ISAGN	I see a great need
ISH	insert sarcasm here
ISLY	I still love you
ISO	in search of
ISS	I said so or I'm so sure
ISSYGTI	I'm so sure you get the idea

ISTM	it seems to me
ISTR	I seem to remember
ISWYM	I see what you mean
ISYALS	I'll send you a letter soon
ITA	I totally agree
ITAM	it's the accounting, man
ITFA	in the final analysis
ITIGBS	I think I'm going to be sick
ITM	in the money
ITS	intense text sex
ITSFWI	if the shoe fits wear it
ITYK	I thought you knew
IUM	if you must
IUSS	if you say so
IWALU	I will always love you
IWBAPTAKYAIYSTA	I will buy a plane ticket and kick your ass if you say that again
IWBNI	it would be nice if
IWIAM	idiot wrapped in a moron
IWIWU	I wish I was you
IWSN	I want sex now
IYAOYAS	if you ain't ordinance you ain't shit
IYD	in your dreams
IYFEG	insert your favorite ethnic group
IYKWIM	if you know what I mean
IYKWIMAITYD	if you know what I mean and I think you do
IYO	in your opinion
IYQ	I like you
IYSS	if you say so
IYSWIM	if you see what I mean

J/C	just checking
J/J	just joking
J/K	just kidding
J/O	jerking off
J/P	just playing
J/W	just wondering
J00	you
J00R	your
J2LYK	just to let you know
J4F	just for fun
J4G	just for grins
J4T OR JFT	just for today
J5M	just five minutes
JAC	just a sec
JAD	just another day
JAFO	just another fucking onlooker
JAFS	just a fucking salesman
JAM	just a minute
JAS	just a second
JC	just curious or just chilling or Jesus Christ
JDI	just do it
JEOMK	just ejaculated on my keyboard
JFH	just fuck her
JFF	just for fun
JFI	just for information
JFGI	just fucking Google it
JIC	just in case
JJA	just joking around
JMY2C	just my 2 cents
JK	just joking
JLMK	just let m know
JMO	just my opinion

JOOTT	just one of those things
JP	just playing or jackpot
JSU	just shut up
JSYK	just so you know
JT	just teasing
JTLYK	just to let you know
JTOL	just thinking out loud
JTOU	just thinking of you
JUADLAM	jumping up and down like a monkey
JW	just wondering

K

K	ok
K8T	Katie
KB	kick butt
KBD	keyboard
KDFU	cracking the fuck up
KEWL	cool
KEYA	I will key you later
KEYME	key me when you get in
KFY or K4Y	kiss for you
KHYF	know how you feel
KIA	killed in action
KIBO	knowledge in, bullshit out
KIR	keep it real
KISS	keep it simple stupid
KIT	keep in touch
KITTY	vagina
KK	kiss kiss or knock knock
KMA	kiss my ass
KMFHA	kiss my fat hairy ass
KMP	keep me posted
KMRIA	kiss my royal Irish arse
KMSLA	kiss my shiny little ass
KMUF	kiss me you fool
KMWA	kiss my white ass
KOC	kiss on cheek
KOK	knock
KOL	kiss on lips
KOTC	kiss on the cheek
KOTL	kiss on the lips
KNIM	know what I mean?
KPC	keeping parents clueless
KS	kill stealer

KUTGW	keep up the good work
KWIM	know what I mean?
KWSTA	kiss with serious tongue action
KYFC	keep your fingers crossed
KYPO	keep your pants on

L

L	laugh
L2G	like to go?
L2G	love to go
L2K	like to come
L33T	leet or elite
L8R	later
L8RG8R	later gator
LABATYD	life's a bitch and then you die
LAQ	lame ass quote
LB?W/C	like bondage whips or chains
LBAY	laughing back at you
LBR and LGR	little boy's room and little girl's room
LBUG or LBIG	laughing because you're gay or laughing because I'm gay
LD	long distance or later dude
LDIMEDILLIGAF	look deeply into my eyes, does it look like I give a fuck
LDR	long distance relationship
LDTTWA	let's do the time warp again
LEMENO	let me know
LERK	leaving easy reach of keyboard
LF	let's fuck
LFG	looking for group or looking for guard
LFTI	looking forward to it
LGH	lets get high
LGMAS	lord give me a sign
LH6	lets have sex
LHM	Lord help me
LHO	laughing head off
LHOS	lets have online sex
LHSO	let's have sex online
LHSX	let's have sex

LIC	like I care
LIFO	last in, first out
LIK	liquor
LIS	laughing in silence
LJBF	let's just be friends
LKITR	little kid in the room
LLOM	like Leno on meth
LLTA	lots and lots of thunderous applause
LMA	leave me alone
LMAO	laughing my ass off
LMBO	laughing my butt off
LMFAO	laughing my fucking ass off
LMHO	laughing my head off
LMIRL	let's meet in real life
LMK	let me know
LMNK	leave my name out
LMSO	laughing my socks off
LMTCB	left message to call back
LOA	list of acronyms
LOL	laughing out loud or lots of love
LOLA	laugh out loud again
LOLH	laughing out loud hysterically
LOLO	lots of love
LOMBARD	lots of money but a right dick
LOML	love of my life
LONH	lights on, nobody home
LOOL	laughing outrageously out loud
LOPSOD	long on promises, short on delivery
LORE	learn once, repeat everywhere
LOTI	laughing on the inside
LOTR	Lord of the Rings
LOU	laughing over you
LPOS	lazy piece of shit
LQTM	laughing quietly to myself
LRF	little rubber feet

LSHMBH	laughing so hard my belly hurts
LSV	language, sex, violence
LTD	living the dream
LTHTT	laughing too hard to type
LTIC	laughing 'til I cry
LTM	laughing to myself
LTNS	long time no see
LTNT	long time, no type
LTOD	laptop of death
LTR	long term relationship
LTS	laughing to self
LTTIC	look the teacher is coming
LULT	love you long time
LULZ	slang for lol
LULU	locally undesirable land use
LUMTP	love you more than pie
LUSM	love you so much
LVM	left voice mail
LWOS	laughing without smiling
LWR	launch when ready
LY	love you
LY4E	love you forever
LYA	love you all
LYB	love you babe
LYCYLBB	love you, see you later, bye bye
LYKYAMY	love you, kiss you, already miss you
LYL	love you lots
LYLAB	love you like a brother
LYLAF	love you like a friend
LYLAS	love you like a sister
LYLB	love you later bye
LYLC	love you like a sis
LYMI	love you, mean it
LYSM	love you so much
LYWAMH	love you with all my heart

M

M2NY	me too, not yet
M4C	meet for coffee
M8 or M8S	mate or mates
MA	mature audience
MAYA	most advanced yet accessible
MB	message board
MBN	must be nice
MBRFN	must be real fucking nice
MC	Merry Christmas
MEGO	my eyes glaze over
MEH	who cares, whatever
MEHH	sigh or sighing
MFD	multi-function device
MFG	mit freundlichen gruessen
MFI	made for it
MFIC	mother fucker in charge
MFWIC	mofo who's in charge
MGB	may God bless
MHBFY	my heart bleeds for you
MHOTY	my hat's off to you
MIA	missing in action
MIHAP	may I have your attention please
MIL	mother-in-law
MILF	mother I'd like to fuck
MIRL	meet in real life
MITIN	more info than I needed
MKAY	mmm ,okay
MKOP	my kind of place
MLA	multiple letter acronym
MLAS	my lips are sealed
MLM	middle finger
MM	market maker or sister

MMHA2U	my most humble apologies to you
MMK	mmm, okay?
MNC	mother nature calls
MNSG	mensaje or message
MO	move on
MOF	matter of fact
MOFO	mother fucker
MOMPL	one moment please
MOO	mud, object-oriented
MOOS	member of the opposite sex
MOP	moment please
MORF	male or female
MOS	mom over shoulder
MOSS	member(s) of the same sex
MOTAS	member of the appropriate sex
MOTD	message of the day
MOTOS	member(s) of the opposite sex
MOTSS	member(s) of the same sex
MP	Mana points
MPFB	my personal fuck buddy
MRA	moving right along
MSG	message
MSMD	monkey see monkey do
MSNUW	mini-skirt no underwear
MTBF	mean time before failure
MTF	more to follow
MTFBWU	may the force be with you
MTFBWY	may the force be with you
MTLA	my true love always
MTSBWY	may the Schwartz be with you
MUAH	the sound of a kiss
MWAH	the sound of a kiss
MUBAR	messed up beyond all recognition
MUSM	miss you so much
MWBRL	more will be revealed later

MYL	mind your language
MYO	mind your own
MYOB	mind your own business

N

N/A	not applicable or not affiliated
N/M	nothing much
N/T	no text
N00B	newbie
N1	nice one
N2m	not to mention or not too much
N2mjchbu	not too much just chillin, how about you
NAB	not a blonde
NADT	not a damn thing
NAGB	nearly almost a good bridge
NAK	nursing at keyboard
NALOPKT	not a lot of people know that
NANA	not now, no need
NATCH	naturally
NAVY	never again volunteer yourself
N-A-Y-L	in a while
NAZ	name, address, zip (also means NASDAQ)
NB4T	not before time
NBD	no big deal
NBFAB	not bad for a beginner
NBFABS	not bad for a bot stopper
NBIF	no basis in fact
NBLFY	nothing but love for you
NC	nice crib
NCG	new college graduate
NDN	Indian or Native American
NE	anyway
NE1	anyone
NE14KFC	anyone for KFC?
NE1ER	anyone here
NE2H	need to have

NESEC	any second
NEV	neighborhood electric vehicle
NEWS	north, east, west, south
NFBSK	not for British school kids
NFC	not favorably considered or no fucking chance
NFF	no fucking fair
NFG	not fucking good
NFI	no fucking idea
NFM	none for me or not for me
NFS	not for sale
NFW	no fucking way or no feasible way
NFWS	not for work safe
NG	new game
NGB	nearly good bridge
NH	nice hand
NHOH	never heard of him/her
NICE	nonsense in crappy existence
NIFOC	nude in front of the computer
NIGI	now I get it
NIGYYSOB	now I've got you, you son of a bitch
NIH	not invented here
NIM	no internal message
NIMBY	not in my back yard
NIMJD	not in my job description
NIMQ	not in my queue
NIMY	never in a million years
NINO	nothing in, nothing out or no input, no output
NIROK	not in reach of keyboard
NISM	need I say more
NITL	not in this lifetime
NIYWFD	not in your wildest fucking dreams
NLL	nice little lady
NLT	no later than

61

NM	never mind or nothing much or nice move
NME	enemy
NMH	not much here
NMHJC	not much here, just chilling
NMP	not my problem
NMTE	now more than ever
NMU	not much, you?
NN	not now
NNCIMINTFZ	not now chief, I'm in the fuckin' zone
NNWW	nudge, nudge, wink, wink
NO	not online
NO1	no one
NOA	not online anymore
NOFI	no offence intended
NOOB	some one who is bad at games
NOS	new old stock
NOY	not online yet
NOYB	none of your business
NP	no problem or nosy parents
NPC	non playing character
NQA	no questions asked
NQT	newly qualified teacher
NQOCD	not quite our class dear
NR	nice roll
NRG	energy
NRN	no reply necessary
NS	nice set
NSA	no strings attached
NSFW	not safe for work
NSISR	not sure if spelled right
NSS	no shit Sherlock
NSTLC	need some tender loving care
NT	nice try
NTA	not this again

NTHING	nothing
NTIM	not that it matters
NTIMM	not that it matters much
NTK	nice to know
NTM	not that much
NTTAWWT	not that there's anything wrong with that
NTW	not to worry
NTYMI	now that you mention it
NUB	new person to a site or game
NUFF	enough said
NVM	never mind
NVR	never
NVNG	nothing ventured, nothing gained
NW	no way
NWAL	nerd without a life
NWO	no way out
NWR	not work related
NYC	not your concern
NYCFS	New York City finger salute

O	opponent or over or hugs
OA	online auctions
OAO	over and out
OATUS	on a totally unrelated subject
OAUS	on an unrelated subject
OB	obligatory or oh baby or oh brother
OBE	overcome by events
OBO	or best offer
OBTW	oh by the way
OBX	old battle axe
OC	original character or own character
OCD	obsessive compulsive disorder
ODTAA	one damn thing after another
OI	operator indisposed
OIC	oh, I see
OICU812	oh I see, you ate one too
OK	all correct
OJ	only joking
OL	old lady
OLL	online love
OLN	online netiquette
OM	old man or oh my
OMB	oh my Buddha
OMDB	over my dead body
OMFG	oh my fucking God
OMFGLMAOBBQROFLCOPTERISS	
	oh my fucking God, laugh my ass off, owned, roll on floor spinning around I'm so sad
OMG	oh my God
OMGYG2BK	oh my God, you got to be kidding
OMIK	open mouth, insert keyboard

OML	oh my lord
OMW	on my way
ONID	oh no I didn't
ONL	online
ONNA	oh no, not again
ONNTA	oh no, not this again
ONUD	oh no you didn't
OO	over and out
OOAK	one of a kind
OOC	out of character or out of control
OOF	out of facility
OOH	out of here
OOI	out of interest
OOO	out of office
OOS	out of stock
OOTB	out of the box or out of the blue
OOTC	obligatory on topic comment
OOTD	one of these days
OOTO	out of the office
OP	on phone
ORLY	oh really?
OSIF	oh shit I forgot
OSINTOT	oh shit I never thought of that
OST	on second thought
OT	off topic
OTASOIC	owing to a slight oversight in construction
OTB	off to bed
OTC	over the counter
OTF	off the floor or on the phone (fone)
OTFL	on the floor laughing
OTH	off the hook
OTL	out to lunch
OTOH	on the other hand
OTP	on the phone

OTT	over the top
OTTOMH	off the top of my head
OTW	off the wall
OUSU	oh, you shut up
OVA	over
OWTTE	or words to that effect
OYO	on you own
OZ	Australia

P	partner
P2P	parent to parent or pat to play
P&C	private & confidential
P2C2E	process too complicated too explain
P2U4URAQTP	peace to you for you are a cutie pie
P911	parent alert
PA	parent alert
PAL	parents are listening
PANS	pretty awesome new stuff
PAW	parents are watching
PB	potty break
PBB	parent behind back
PBEM	play by email
PBJ	peanut butter and jelly or pretty boy jock
PBOOK	phonebook
PC	player character
PCM	please call me
PD	public domain
PDH	pretty darn happy
PDOMA	pulled directly out of my ass
PDQ	pretty darn quick
PDS	please don't shout
PEBCAC	problem exists between chair and computer
PEBCAK	problem exists between chair and keyboard
PEEPS	people
PFA	pulled from ass or please find attached
PFC	pretty fucking cold
PHAT	pretty hot and tempting
PHB	pointy haired boss

PHS	pointy haired stupidvisor
PIAPS	pig in a pant suit
PIBKAC	problem is between keyboard and chair
PICNIC	problem in chair, not in computer
PIF	paid in full
PIMP	peeing in my pants
PIMPL	peeing in my pants laughing
PIN	person in need
PIP	peeing in pants
PIR	parent in room
PISS	put in some sugar
PITA	pain in the ass
PITMEMBOAM	peace in the Middle East my brother of another mother
PKMN	Pokemon
PL8	plate
PLMK	please let me know
PLO	peace, love, out
PLOKTA	press lots of keys to abort
PLOS	parents looking over shoulder
PLS	please
PLU	people like us or you
PLZ	please
PM	personal message or private message
PMBI	pardon my butting in
PMF	pardon my French or pure fucking magic
PMFI	pardon me for interrupting
PMFJI	pardon me for jumping in
PMIGBOM	put mind in gear before opening mouth
PMJI	pardon my jumping in
PML	pissing myself laughing
PMP	peeing my pants
PMSL	pissed myself laughing

PNATMBC	pay no attention to man behind the curtain
PNCAH	please, no cursing allowed here
PND	possibly not definitely or personal navigation device
PO	piss off
POAHF	put on a happy face
POAK	passed out at keyboard
POM	parent over my shoulder
PONA	person of no account
POP	piece of paper
POOF	goodbye, gone; also seen as ::poof::
POS	parent over shoulder or piece of shit
POSC	piece of shit computer
POSSLQ	persons of the opposite sex sharing living quarters
POTS	plain old telephone system or pat on the shoulder
POTUS	president of the United States
POV	point of view
PP	people
PPL	pay per lead or people
PPU	pending pick up
PROLLY	probably
PRON	pornography
PRT	party
PRW	parents are watching
PS	post script
PSA	public service announcement
PSO	product superior to Operator
PSOS	parent standing over shoulder
PSP	Playstation Portable
PST	please send tell
PTH	prime tanning hours
PTL	Praise the Lord

PTMM	please tell me more
PTP	pardon the pun
PTPOP	pat the pissed off primate
PU	that stinks
PUG	pick up group
PUKS	pick up kids
PVP	player versus player
PWN	own
PWNT	owned
PWP	plot, what plot?
PXT	please explain that
PZ	peace
P-ZA	pizza

Q

Q	queue
Q2C	quick to cum
QFE	question for everyone
QFI	quoted for idiocy or irony
QFT	quoted for truth or quit fucking talking
QIK	quick
QL	quit laughing
QLS	reply
QOTD	quote of the day
QQ	quick question or cry more
QS	quit scrolling
QSL	reply
QSO	conversation
QT	cutie
QTPI	cutie pie
QYB	quit your bitching

R

R	are
R8	rate
R/U/S	are you serious?
R U THERE?	are you there?
R&D	research & development
R&R	rest & relaxation
RAEBNC	read and enjoyed but no comment
RAT	remotely activated Trojan
RB@YA	right back at ya
RBAY	right back at you
RBTL	read between the lines
RC	remote control
RCI	rectal cranial inversion
RE	regards or reply or hello again
REHI	hi again
RFD	request for discussion
RFR	really fucking rich
RFS	really fucking soon
RGR	roger
RHIP	rank has its privileges
RIP	rest in peace
RIYL	recommended if you like
RKBA	right to keep and bear arms
RL	real life
RLCO	real life conference
RLF	real life friend
RLY	really
RM	remake
RME	rolling my eyes
RMLB	read my lips baby
RMMA	reading my mind again
RMMM	read my mail man

RN	right now
RNN	reply not necessary
ROFL	rolling on floor laughing
ROFLCOPTR	rolling on floor laughing and spinning around
ROR	raffing out roud (in Scooby-doo dialect)
ROTFL	rolling on the floor laughing
ROTFLOL	rolling on the floor laughing out loud
ROTFLMAO	rolling on the floor laughing my ass off
ROTFLMFAO	rolling on the floor laughing my fucking ass off
ROTFLOL	rolling on the floor laughing out loud
ROTFLUTS	rolling on the floor laughing unable to speak
ROTGL	rolling on the ground laughing
ROTGLMAO	rolling on the ground laughing my ass off
ROTM	right on the money
RPG	role playing games
RRQ	return receipt request
RRR	har har har (instead of lol)
RS	Runscape
RSN	real soon now
RSVP	répondez s'il vous plaît
RT	real time
RTBM	read the bloody manual
RTBS	reason to be single
RTFAQ	read the faq
RTFF	read the fucking faq
RTFM	read the fucking manual
RTFQ	read the fucking question
RTH	release the hounds
RTK	return to keyboard
RTM or RTFM	read the manual or read the fucking manual
RTNTN	retention

RTSM	read the silly manual
RTTSD	right thing to say dude
RTWFQ	read the whole fucking question
RU	are you?
RUT	are you there?
RU/18	are you over 18?
RUFKM	are you fucking kidding me?
RUH	are you horny?
RUOK	are you okay?
RUMCYMHMD	are you on medication cause you must have missed a dose
RUMORF	are you male or female?
RUNTS	are you nuts?
RUOK	are you ok?
RUS	are you serious?
RUSOS	are you SOS (in trouble)?
RUT	are you there?
RUUP4IT	are you up for it?
RX	regards
RYFM	read your friendly Manual
RYB	read your Bible
RYO	roll your own
RYS	read your screen

S

S	smile
S^	what's up?
S2R	send to receive
S2S	sorry to say
S2U	same to you
S4L	spam for life
SADAD	suck a dick and die
SAHM	stay at home mom
SAIA	stupid asses in action
SAL	such a laugh
SAPFU	surpassing all previous foul ups
SB	stand by
SBI	sorry 'bout it
SBT	sorry 'bout that
SBTA	sorry, being thick again
SBUG	small bald unaudacious Goal
SC	stay cool
SCNR	sorry, could not resist
SDK	Scottie doesn't know or software developer's kit
SDMB	sweet dreams my baby
SEC	wait a second
SED	said enough darling
SEG	shit eating grin
SEP	somebody else's problem
SETE	smiling ear to ear
SEWAG	scientifically engineered wild ass guess
SF	surfer friendly or science fiction
SFAIAA	so far as I am aware
SFAIK	so far as I know
SFETE	smiling from ear to ear
SFLA	stupid four letter acronym

SFTTM	stop fucking talking to me
SFX	sound effects or stage effects
SH	shit happens or same here
SH^	shut up
SHB	should have been
SHID	slap head in disgust
SHMILY	see how much I love you
SIC	spelling is correct
SICL	sitting in chair laughing
SICS	sitting in chair snickering
SICNR	sorry, I got to run
SIHTH	stupidity is hard to take
SII	seriously impaired imagination
SIL	sister-in-law
SIMYC	sorry I missed your call
SIP	skiing in powder
SIS	snickering in silence
SIT	stay in touch
SITCOMS	single income, two children, oppressive mortgage
SITD	still in the dark
SIUP	suck it up pussy
SIUYA	shove it up your ass
SK8	skate
SK8NG	skating
SK8R	skater
SK8RBOI	skater boy
SL	second life
SLAP	sounds like a plan
SLAW	sounds like a winner
SLIRK	smart little rich kid
SLM	see last mail
SLOM	sticking leeches on myself
SLT	something like that
SM	senior moment

SMAIM	send me an instant message
SMB	suck my balls
SME	subject matter expert
SMEM	send me e-mail
SMH	shaking my head
SMHID	scratching my head in disbelief
SMIM	send me an instant message
SMOP	small matter of programming
SNAFU	situation normal, all fucked up
SNAG	sensitive new age guy
SNERT	snotty nosed egotistical rotten teenager
SO	significant other (spouse, boy/girlfriend)
SOAB	son of a bitch
SOB	son of a bitch
SOBT	stressed out big time
SOGOP	shit or get off the pot
SOH	sense of humor
SOHF	sense of humor failure
SOI	self owning idiot
SOIAR	sit on it and rotate
SOL	shit out of luck or sooner or later
SOMY	sick of me yet?
SorG	straight or gay?
SOOYA	snake out of your ass
SOP	standard operating procedure
SORG	straight or gay
SOS	same old shit or help
SOT	short on time
SOTMG	short on time must go
SOW	speaking of which or statement of work
SOWM	someone with me
SOZ	sorry
SPK	speak
SRO	standing room only
SRSLY	seriously

SPST	same place same time
SPTO	spoke to
SQ	square
SRY	sorry
SS	so sorry
SSC	super sexy cute
SSDD	same shit different day!
SSEWBA	someday soon, everything will be acronyms
SSIA	subject says it all
SSIF	so stupid it's funny
SSINF	so stupid it's not funny
STBY	sucks to be you
ST&D	stop texting and drive
STD	seal the deal or sexually transmitted disease
STFU	shut the fuck up
STFW	search the fucking web
STM	spank the monkey
STPPYNOZGTW	stop picking your nose, get to work
STR8	straight
STS	so to speak
STW	search the web
STYS	speak to you soon
SU	shut up
SUAC	shit up a creek
SUAKM	shut up and kiss me
SUFI	super finger or shut up fucking imbecile
SUFID	screwing up face in Disgust
SUITM	s you in the morning
SUL	snooze you lose or see you later
SUP	what's up?
SUYF	shut up you fool
SWAG	scientific wild ass guess -and- software and giveaways

SWAK	sealed (or sent) with a kiss
SWALBCAKWS	sealed with a lick because a kiss won't stick
SWALK	sealed with a loving kiss
SWAT	scientific wild ass guess
SWDYT	so what do you think?
SWIM	see what I mean?
SWIS	see what I'm saying?
SWL	screaming with laughter
SWMBO	she who must be obeyed
SWU	so what's up?
SYL	see you later
SYS	see you soon
SYT	see you tomorrow

T

T+	think positive
T:)T	think happy thoughts
T&C	terms & conditions
T@YL	talk at you later
TA	thanks again or a lot
TABOOMA	take a bite out of my ass
TAF	that's all, folks!
TAFN	that's all for now
TAH	take a hike
TAKS	that's a knee slapper
TANJ	there ain't no justice
TANK	really strong
TANKED	owned
TANKING	owning
TANSTAAFL	there ain't no such thing as a free lunch
TAM	tomorrow a.m.
TAP	take a pill
TARFU	things are really fucked up
TAS	taking a shower
TAU	thinking about you
TAUMUALU	thinking about you miss you always love you
TAW	teachers are watching
TBA	to be advised
TBAG	process of disgracing a corpse, taunting a fragged / killed player
TBC	to be continued
TBD	to be determined
TBE	thick between ears
TBH	to be honest
TBL	txt back later
TBYB	try before you buy

TC	take care
TCB	trouble came back
TCOY	take care of yourself
TD	tower defense
TDM	too darn many
TDTM	talk dirty to me
TEOTWAWKI	the end of the world as we know it
TFDS	that is for darn sure
TFH	thread from hell
TFLMS	thanks for letting me share
TFMIU	the fucking manual is unreadable
TFN	thanks for nothing or til further notice
TFS	thanks for sharing or three finger salute
TFTHAOT	thanks for the help ahead of time
TFTT	thanks for the thought
TFX	traffic
TGAL	think globally, act locally
TGGTG	that girl/guy has got to go
TGIF	thank god it's Friday
THX or TX or THKS	thanks
THT	think happy thoughts
THNQ	thank you
TIA	thanks in advance
TIAD	tomorrow is another day
TIAIL	think I am in love
TIC	tongue in cheek
TIGAS	think I give a shit
TILII	tell it like it is
TILIS	tell it like it is
TINWIS	that is not what I said
TISC	this is so cool
TISL	this is so lame
TISNC	this is so not cool
TISNF	that is so not fair
TISNT	that is so not true

TK	to come
TKU4UK	thank you for your Kindness
TL	too long
TLA	three letter acronym
TLC	tender loving care
TLGO	the list goes on
TLITBC	that's life in the big city
TLK2UL8R	talk to you later
TLK-2-U-L-8-R	talk to you later
TM	trust me
TMA	too many acronyms
TMB	text me back
TMI	too much information
TMOT	trust me on this
TMTH	to much to handle
TMTOWTDI	there's more than one way to do it
TMWFI	take my word for it
TNA	temporarily not available
TNC	tongue in cheek
TNT	till next time
TNTL	trying not to laugh
TNX	thanks
TNSTAAFL	there's no such thing as a free lunch
TNT	till next time
TOBAL	there oughta be a law
TOBG	this oughta be good
TOJ	tears of joy
TOM	tomorrow
TOPCA	till our paths cross again
TOT	tons of time
TOU	thinking of you
TOY	thinking of you
TP	team player or teleport
TPC	the phone company
TPM	tomorrow p.m.

TPS	that's pretty stupid
TPTB	the powers that be
TQ	te quiero / I love you
TQM	total quality management
TRAM	the rest are mine
TRDMC	tears running down my cheeks
TS	tough shit or totally stinks
TSIA	this says it all
TSIF	thank science it's Friday
TSNF	that's so not fair
TSOB	tough son of a bitch
TSR	totally stuck in ram or totally stupid rules
TSRA	two shakes of a rat's ass
TSTB	the sooner the better
TT	big tease
TTA	tap that ass
TTBOMK	to the best of my knowledge
TTFN	ta ta for now
TTG	time to go
TTIOT	the truth is out there
TTKSF	trying to keep a straight face
TTMF	ta ta mofo
TTS	text to speech
TTT	that's the ticket or to the top or thought that too
TTTHTFAL	talk to the hand the face ain't listening
TTTKA	time to totally kick ass
TTTT	to tell the truth
TTUL	talk to you later
TTYAWFN	talk to you a while from now
TTYL	talk to you later or type to you later
TTYS	talk to you soon
TTYT	talk to you tomorrow
TVM4YEM	thank you very much for your e-mail
TVN	thank you very much

TWHAB	this won't hurt a bit
TWIMC	to whom it may concern
TWIWI	that was interesting, wasn't it?
TXS	thanks
TXT IM	text instant message
TY	thank you
TYCLO	turn your caps lock off
TYSO	thank you so much
TYVM	thank you very much

U

^URS	up yours
U	you
U UP	are you up?
U2	you too
U8	you ate?
UBS	unique buying state
UCMU	you crack me up
UCWAP	up a creek without a paddle
UDH82BME	you'd hate to be me
UDI	unidentified drinking injury
UDM	u da man
UFB	unfucking believable
UFN	until further notice
UG2BK	you've got to be kidding
UGTBK	you've got to be kidding
UGC	user-generated content
UKTR	you know that's right
U-L	you will
UL	upload
UN4TUN8	unfortunate
UNBLEFBLE	unbelievable
UNCRTN	uncertain
UNPC	un-politically correct
UNTCO	you need to chill out
UOK	are you ok?
UPOD	under promise over deliver
UR	you are
UR2K	you are too kind
UR2YS4ME	you are to wise for me
URA*	you are a star
URAPITA	you are a pain in the ass
URH	you are hot

URSAI	you are such an idiot
URSKTM	you are so kind to me
URTM	you are the man
URW	you are welcome
URWS	you are wise
URYY4M	you are too wise for me
US	you suck
USP	unique selling
USU	usually Proposition
UT	unreal tournament
UT2L	you take too long
UTM	you tell me
UV	unpleasant visual
UW	you're welcome
UWIWU	you wish I was you

V

VBG	very big grin
VBS	very big smile
VC	venture capital
VCDA	vaya con dios, amigo
VEG	very evil grin
VFF	very fucking funny
VFM	value for money
VGG	very good game
VGH	very good hand
VGN	vegan or vegetarian
VIP	very important person
VM	voice mail
VN	very nice
VNH	very nice hand
VRBS	virtual reality bull shit
VRY	very
VSC	very soft chuckle
VSF	very sad face
VWD	very well done
VWP	very well played

W

W/	with
W/O	without
W@	what?
W00T	we own the other team
W3	www or world wide web
W8	wait
WAD	without a doubt
WAEF	when all else fails
WAFB	what a fucking bitch
WAFM	what a fucking mess
WAFS	warm and fuzzies
WAG	wild ass guess
WAH	working at home
WAI	what an idiot
WAJ	what a jerk
WAK	what a kiss
WAM	wait a minute
WAMBAM	web application meets brick and mortar
WAN2	want 2?
WAN2TLK	want to talk
WAREZ	pirated
WAS	wait a second or wild ass guess
WAWA	where are we at?
WAYD	what are you doing?
WAYF	where are you from?
WAYN	where are you now?
WB	welcome back or write back
WBS	write back soon
WBU	what about you?
WC	who cares
WCA	who cares anyway

Wd	well done
WDALYIC	who died and left you in charge?
WDDD	woopie doo da dey
WDR	with due respect
WDT	who does that?
WDYMBT	what do you mean by that?
WDYS	what did you say?
WDYT	what do you think?
WE	whatever
W/END	weekend
WEG	wicked evil grin
WEP	weapon
WETSU	we eat this shit up
WF	way fun
WFM	works for me
WG	wicked grin
WGAFF	who gives a flying fuck
WH5	who, what, where, when, why
WIBAMU	well, I'll be a monkey's uncle
WIBNI	wouldn't it be nice if
WIIFM	what's in it for me?
WILCO	will comply
WIM	woe is me
WIP	work in process
WISP	winning is so pleasurable
WIT	wordsmith in training
WITFITS	what in the fuck is this shit
WITW	what in the world
WIU	wrap it up
WK	week
WKD	weekend
WKEWL	way cool
WMHGB	where many have gone before
WMMOWS	wash my mouth out with soap
WMPL	wet my pants laughing

WNOHGB	where no one has gone before
WOA	work of art
WOG	wise old guy
WOMBAT	waste of money, brains and time
WOOF	well off older folks
WOP	with out papers
WOTAM	waste of time and money
WOTD	word of the day
WOW	world of warcraft
WP	well played
WRK	work
WRT	with regard to or with respect to
WRU@	where are you at?
WRUD	what are you doing?
WRUDATM	what are you doing at the moment?
WT	without thinking or what the or who the
WTB	want to buy
WTF	what the fuck?
WTFE	what the fuck ever
WTFO	what the fuck? over
WTFGDA	way to fucking go, dumb ass
WTFH	what the fucking hell
WTG	way to go
WTGP	want to go private?
WTH	what the heck
WTHOW	white trash headline of the week
WTMI	way too much information
WTN	what then now? Who then now?
WTS	want to sell
WTSDS	where the sun don't shine
WTSHTF	when the shit hits the fan
WTT	want to trade?
WTTM	without thinking to much
WU?	what's up
WUF	where you from

WUCIWUG	what you see is what you get
WUF?	Where are you from?
WUU2	what are you up to?
WUW	what u want?
WUWH	wish you were here
WUWHIMA	wish you were here in my arms
WWJD	what would Jesus do?
WWNC	will wonders never cease
WWSD	what would Satan do?
WWY	where were you?
WX	weather
WYCM	will you call me?
WYD	what you doing?
WYFM	would you fuck me?
WYGAM	when you get a minute
WYGISWYPF	what you get is what you pay for
WYHAM	when you have a minute
WYLEI	when you last expect it
WYM	what do you mean?
WYP	what's your problem?
WYRN	what's your real name?
WYS	whatever you say
WYSILOB	what you see is a load of bullocks
WYSIWYG	what you see is what you get
WYSLPG	what you see looks pretty good
WYT	whatever you think
WYWH	wish you were here

X

X	kiss
X!	typical woman
X-I-10	exciting
XD	devilish smile or really hard laugh
XLNT	excellent
XME	excuse me
XOXO	hugs and kisses
XQZT	exquisite
XTC	ecstasy
XYL	wife

Y

Y?	why?
Y2K	you're too kind
YA	yet another
YA YAYA	yet another yaya (as in yoyo)
YABA	yet another bloody acronym
YACC	yet another calendar company
YAFIYGI	you asked for it you got it
YAOTM	yet another off topic message
YAELY	ya, really?
YAUN	yet another Unix nerd
YBIC	your brother in Christ
YBF	you've been fucked
YBS	you'll be sorry
YBY	yeah baby yeah
YBYSA	you bet your sweet ass
YCLIU	you can look it up
YCMU	you crack me up
YCT	your comment to
YDKM	you don't know me
YEPPIES	young experimenting perfection seekers
YF	wife
YG	young
YGBK	you gotta be kidding
YGBSM	you gotta be shiting me
YGG	you go girl
YGLT	you're gonna love this
YGTBKM	you've got to be kidding me
YGWYPF	you get what you pay for
YHM	you have mail
YIC	yours in Christ
YIU	yes, I understand
YIWGP	yes, I will go private

YKW	you know what
YKWIM	you know what I mean
YKWYCD	you know what you can do
YL	young lady
YM	your mother
YMAK	you may already know
YMMV	your mileage may vary
YNK	you never know
YOYO	you're on your own
YR	yeah right or your
YRYOCC	you're running on your own cuckoo clock
YS	you stinker
YSAN	you're such a nerd
YSIC	why should I care?
YSK	you should know
YSYD	yeah, sure you do
YT	you there?
YTB	you're the best
YTG	you're the greatest
YTRNW	yeah that's right, now
YTTL	you take to long
YTTT	you telling the truth
YUPPIES	young urban professionals
YW	you're welcome
YW	you're wrong
YWHNB	yes, we have no bananas
YWIA	you're welcome in advance
YWSYLS	you win some you lose some
YY4U	too wise for you
YYSSW	yeah yeah sure sure whatever

Z

Z	zero or going to sleep or said
Z%	zoo
ZERG	to gang up on someone
ZH	sleeping hour
ZMG	oh my god
ZOT	zero tolerance
ZUP	what's up?
ZZZZ	sleeping, bored, tired

* 9 7 8 1 4 4 1 4 2 2 6 3 7 *